Beginner Piano Elements for Adults

Book & Videos   Level 1   Damon Ferrante

Introduction

How the Book Works

> ❖Check Out
> Video Lesson 1:
> Introduction

The Book

This beginner book and video course follows a step-by-step lesson format for learning how to play the piano. It is designed for adult beginners and no music experience or music reading is necessary to use the book. Each lesson builds on the previous one in a clear and easy-to-understand manner. You learn how to play the piano through famous songs and pieces.

Beginner Piano Elements for Adults, Level 1, is the first part of a piano book and video instruction series by Damon Ferrante, professor of Piano Studies. At the end of the book, you will be able to play the following songs and pieces in easy-piano arrangements: *Jingle Bells, Ode to Joy, When the Saints Go Marching In, Yankee Doodle, Take Me Out to the Ballgame, Beethoven 5th Symphony,* and many more.

The Videos

There are Free, Streaming Video Lessons that coincide with the material presented in *Piano Elements*. The Lesson Videos cover playing songs and pieces, piano technique, how to read music, and basic music concepts. All of these videos are <u>free</u> and available on <u>Youtube</u> type "**Piano Elements Book**". <u>No</u> Registration or Sign-Up is needed to view the videos and there is no limit to the amount of times that they may be viewed.

Table of Contents

Beginner Piano Elements for Adults:
Teach Yourself to Play Piano, Step-By-Step Guide
to Get You Started, Level 1
(Book & Videos)

by Damon Ferrante

For additional information about
music books, recordings, and concerts,
please visit the Steeplechase website:
www.steeplechasearts.com

steepLechase

arts & productions

ISBN-13:
978-0615936154 (Steeplechase Arts)

ISBN-10:
0615936156

Right Hand

RH

Chapter 1

Lesson 1: Hand Position & Finger Numbers

- To create a good hand position for piano playing is easy. With both hands, imagine that you are holding an apple (with your palms facing upward and your fingers curved). Then, turn your palms to the floor and keep your fingers curved. **See Video Lesson 1**
- For piano playing, our fingers are given numbers. The numbers are the same for both hands. **See Video Lesson 1**

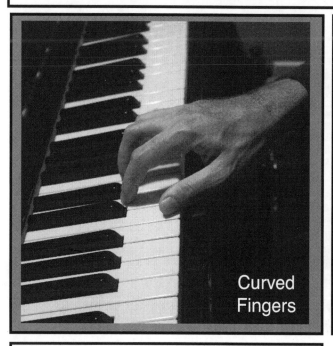

Curved Fingers

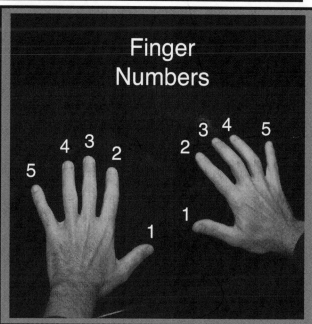

Finger Numbers

- RH stands for Right Hand.
- LH stands for Left Hand.

Finger Numbers
- Thumb = Finger #1
- Pointer = Finger #2
- Middle = Finger #3
- Ring = Finger #4
- Pinky = Finger #5

The finger numbers are the same for both hands. For example, the thumb is finger #1 in both the right hand and left hand and the pinky is finger #5 in both hands.

For Video Lesson 1, type "Piano Elements Book" into Youtube.

Lesson 2: Middle C & Good Posture at the Piano

- On the Piano Keyboard, you might notice that there are 2 sets of keys: Black and White Keys. The Black Keys are in groups of 2 and 3 keys.
- If you look near the middle of the piano keyboard, you will see a set of 2 Black Keys. The White Key, directly to the Left of this set of 2 Black Keys (near the middle of the piano keyboard) is called "Middle C".
- Middle C is an important reference note on the piano. We will be playing it in many of our songs.
- For some help in locating Middle C on the piano, **See Video Lesson 1.**

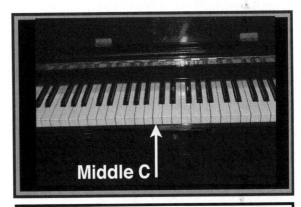

Middle C

From the beginning of your piano playing, it is important to practice good posture: keep your back straight and your arms and shoulders relaxed.

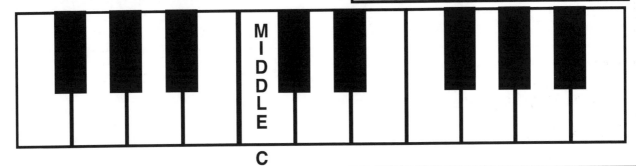

M
I
D
D
L
E
C

Exercises:
- Try Locating Middle C with Finger #1 (Thumb) of your Right Hand (RH)
- Try Locating Middle C with Finger #1 (Thumb) of your Left Hand (LH)

Lesson 3: Keyboard Notes

- The White Keys on the piano follow an alphabetic pattern that goes from A to G. In other words, this is the pattern: A, B, C, D, E, F, G.
- This pattern starts at the bottom (low bass notes) of the piano keyboard and repeats many times as the notes go upward and get higher in pitch ("sound").
- With your RH ("Right Hand") Index Finger, find the "A" key just 2 keys below MIddle C (See the Chart below). Move your Index Finger up (to the right) one key at a time. Try saying the letters as you press down each key. **See Video Lesson 1**

Down
(Lower Pitch)

Up
(Higher Pitch)

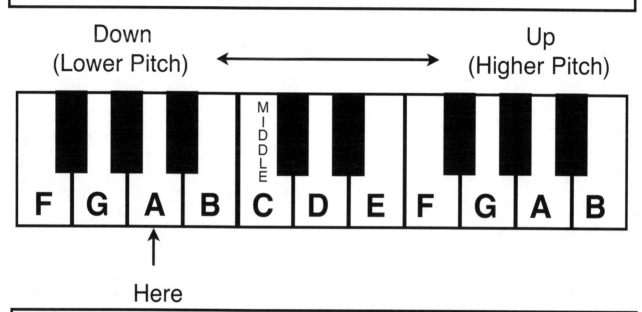

Here

- It is a good idea to associate each key with some object and imagine the object on top of the key. This will help you remember the name and location of each key.
- For this exercise, let's image that the piano keyboard is a table with food on it. The food, on this imagined table, will be placed in a set order going from left to right (See the chart below). Find the key "A" below Middle C and name the foods as you move upward (right). When you get to the second key "A", the pattern will repeat. Repeat this exercise.

White Keys Exercise: A= Apple, B= Bread, C= Cheese, D= Dessert, E= Eggs, F= Fish, G= Grapes

Exercises:
- Try Locating Middle C with Finger #1 (Thumb) of your Right Hand (RH)
- Try Locating Middle C with Finger #1 (Thumb) of your Left Hand (LH)
- Try Locating D with Finger #2 (Pointer Finger) of your Right Hand (RH)
- Try Locating E with Finger #3 (Middle Finger) of your Right Hand (RH)
- Try Locating G with Finger #5 (Pinky Finger) of your Right Hand (RH)

Lesson 4: Three-Note Songs, Using the Right Hand ("RH")

- Try these songs, which use the notes C, D, and E in the right hand ("RH").
- In your right hand, use Thumb for Middle C, use Pointer for D, and use Middle Finger for E.
- Take a look at the keyboard chart and photo below and practice each song 5-10 times.
- As an extra bonus, try saying the letter names aloud as you play each song. This will help you associate the note name with the key and finger number.

RH

MIDDLE
C D E

Notes:

Finger Numbers: 1 2 3

C, D, and E in the Right Hand

Springtime

RH: 1 1 1 1 | 2 2 2 2 | 3 3 3 3 | 2 2 1 1 ‖
    C C C C | D D D D | E E E E | D D C C ‖

Dancing

RH: 1 1 2 2 | 1 1 3 3 | 1 1 2 2 | 1 1 1 1 ‖
    C C D D | C C E E | C C D D | C C C C ‖

Lesson 5: More Three-Note Songs Using the Right Hand

• Try these songs, which also use the notes C, D, and E in the right hand ("RH").

RH

Notes:
Finger Numbers:

C	1
D	2
E	3

Try saying the notes aloud as you play each song.

The double lines (called the "Double Bar") indicate the end of a song or piece.

Jazz Dance

RH: 2 2 1 1 | 2 2 3 3 | 2 2 1 2 | 2 2 1 2 ‖
    D D C C | D D E E | D D C D | D D C D

Blue Sky

RH: 3 2 3 1 | 2 2 2 2 | 3 2 3 1 | 2 2 1 1 ‖
    E D E C | D D D D | E D E C | D D C C

Soccer Fun

RH: 1 1 3 3 | 2 2 3 3 | 1 1 3 3 | 2 2 1 1 ‖
    C C E E | D D E E | C C E E | D D C C

Lesson 6: Counting & Measures

- Music is composed of groups of beats called measures.
- Measures are set off by vertical lines, called bar lines.
- Measures most commonly contain 2, 3, or 4 beats.
- Below, are examples of sets of four measures in 4/4 time.
- In 4/4 time, you will count 4 beats for each measure.
  In other words, you will count: 1234, 1234, 1234, 1234.
- Try counting aloud and clapping the beats for the exercise below.

See Video Lesson 2

Example 1:

| 1 2 3 4 | 1 2 3 4 | 1 2 3 4 | 1 2 3 4 ||

Example 2:
Try Clapping on the X: On the First Beat.

| 1 2 3 4 | 1 2 3 4 | 1 2 3 4 | 1 2 3 4 ||
| X | X | X | X |

Example 3:
Try Clapping on the X: On the First and Third Beats.

| 1 2 3 4 | 1 2 3 4 | 1 2 3 4 | 1 2 3 4 ||
| X   X | X   X | X   X | X   X |

Example 4:
Try Clapping on the X: On the Second Beat.

| 1 2 3 4 | 1 2 3 4 | 1 2 3 4 | 1 2 3 4 ||
| X | X | X | X |

Lesson 7: Counting along with Three-Note Songs (RH)

- Try counting aloud (1234) for each measure, while playing these songs. The songs use the notes C, D, and E in the right hand ("RH"): Fingers 1, 2, and 3. *Have fun!*

RH

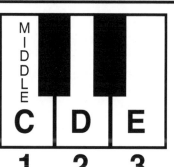

Notes:

Finger Numbers: **1   2   3**

*The Numbers in these songs are for the <u>Beats</u>, <u>not</u> the Finger Numbers.

Summer Rock

Beats:	**1**	**2**	**3**	**4**	**1**	**2**	**3**	**4**	**1**	**2**	**3**	**4**	**1**	**2**	**3**	**4**
	D	D	C	D	D	D	C	D	E	E	D	D	E	E	D	D

A Short Walk

Beats:	**1**	**2**	**3**	**4**	**1**	**2**	**3**	**4**	**1**	**2**	**3**	**4**	**1**	**2**	**3**	**4**
	C	C	C	C	D	D	D	D	E	E	D	D	C	C	C	C

When's Dessert?

Beats:	**1**	**2**	**3**	**4**	**1**	**2**	**3**	**4**	**1**	**2**	**3**	**4**	**1**	**2**	**3**	**4**
	E	D	C	C	D	D	E	E	D	D	C	D	E	D	C	C

Lesson 8: 5-Note Songs Right Hand (RH)

- Let's add 2 new notes for the right hand ("RH"): F and G.
- F will be played with the 4th finger (Ring Finger).
- G will be played with the 5th finger (Pinky Finger).

RH

Notes: **C D E F G**

Finger Numbers: **1 2 3 4 5**

The numbers here are for <u>beats</u>, not fingers. When there is a blank space, don't play for that beat or beats.

↑ ↑ — New Notes

Mary's Little Lamb

Beats:	1	2	3	4		1	2	3	4		1	2	3	4		1	2	3	4
	E	D	C	D		E	E	E			D	D	D			E	G	G	
	Ma-	ry	had	a		lit-	tle	lamb,			lit-	tle	lamb,			lit-	tle	lamb.	

Jingle Bells

Beats:	1	2	3	4		1	2	3	4		1	2	3	4		1	2	3	4
	E	E	E			E	E	E			E	G	C	D		E			
	Jin-	gle	Bells,			Jin-	gle	Bells,			Jin-	gle	all	the		way.			

Beats:	1	2	3	4		1	2	3	4		1	2	3	4		1	2	3	4
	F	F	F	F		F	E	E	E		E	D	D	E		D		G	
	Oh!	What	fun	it		is	to	ride	in		a	one-horse	open	sleigh!		Hey!			

Lesson 9: More 5-Note Songs for the Right Hand (RH)

- Here are a few more songs that use the five fingers of the right hand.
- Remember to find Middle C with the Thumb of your right hand (RH).

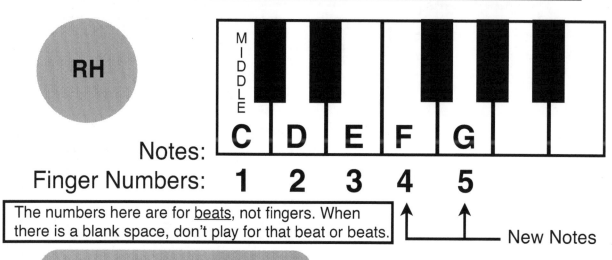

RH

Notes: C D E F G

Finger Numbers: **1 2 3 4 5**

The numbers here are for <u>beats</u>, not fingers. When there is a blank space, don't play for that beat or beats.

New Notes

Starlight

Beats:	**1**	**2**	**3**	**4**		**1**	**2**	**3**	**4**		**1**	**2**	**3**	**4**		**1**	**2**	**3**	**4**	
	F	E	D	C		G	G	G	G		F	E	D	C		G	G	C	C	

Ode to Joy

Beats:	**1**	**2**	**3**	**4**		**1**	**2**	**3**	**4**		**1**	**2**	**3**	**4**		**1**	**2**	**3**	**4**
	E	E	F	G		G	F	E	D		C	C	D	E		E	D	D	

Beats:	**1**	**2**	**3**	**4**		**1**	**2**	**3**	**4**		**1**	**2**	**3**	**4**		**1**	**2**	**3**	**4**	
	E	E	F	G		G	F	E	D		C	C	D	E		D	C	C		

Lesson 10: Chapter 1
What We Have Learned

- Finger Numbers: 1, 2, 3, 4, and 5
- Right-Hand & Left-Hand Abbreviations: RH & LH
- Good Piano Technique: Curved Fingers
- Finding Middle C
- Counting and Measures
- Naming the Notes While Playing Songs
- Counting the Beats While Playing Songs

Check Out These Artists, Songs, and Pieces

- Beethoven: *Für Elise*
- Billy Joel: *The Piano Man*
- Ray Charles: *Georgia On My Mind*
- Vanessa Carlton: *A Thousand Miles*
- Chopin: *The Minute Waltz*

Left Hand

Chapter 2

Lesson 11: Three-Note Songs, Using the Left Hand ("LH")

- Try these songs, which use the notes A, B, and Middle C in the left hand ("LH").
- In your left hand, use Thumb for Middle C, use Pointer for B, and use Middle Finger for A.
- Take a look at the keyboard chart and photo below and practice each song 5-10 times.
- As an extra bonus, try saying the letter names aloud as you play each song. This will help you associate the note name with the key and finger number. ***Have Fun!***

Notes: A   B   C
Finger Numbers: 3   2   1

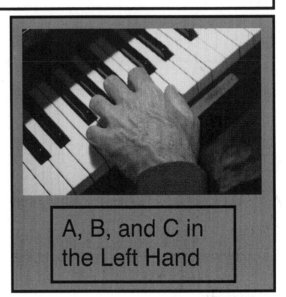

A, B, and C in the Left Hand

The numbers here are for <u>fingers</u>, not beats.

In Winter

LH: **1 1 2 3** | **1 1 2 3** | **2 2 3 3** | **2 2 3 3** ‖
     C C B A | **C C B A** | **B B A A** | **B B A A**

A Mystery

LH: **3 2 1 2** | **3 2 1 2** | **1 1 3 3** | **1 2 3 3** ‖
     A B C B | **A B C B** | **C C A A** | **C B A A**

Lesson 12: More Three-Note Songs Using the Left Hand

• Try these songs, which also use the notes A, B, and C in the Left hand ("LH").

LH

Notes:

| A | B | C (MIDDLE) |

Finger Numbers: **3   2   1**

The numbers here are for <u>fingers</u>, not beats.

Try saying the notes aloud as you play each song.

Moments

LH:
| 2 3 2 3 | 1 1 1 1 | 2 3 2 3 | 1 1 3 3 ‖
| B A B A | C C C C | B A B A | C C A A

Clouds

LH:
| 1 3 2 1 | 1 3 2 1 | 2 2 3 3 | 1 2 3 3 ‖
| C A B C | C A B C | B B A A | C B A A

The Storm

LH:
| 1 3 1 3 | 2 3 2 3 | 1 3 1 3 | 2 2 3 3 ‖
| C A C A | B A B A | C A C A | B B A A

Lesson 13: Time Signatures

- Measures are composed of groups of beats called Time Signatures or Meter (both terms mean the same thing and are interchangeable).
- The most common Time Signatures (or "meters") are groups of 2, 3, or 4 beats per measure: 2/4, 3/4, and 4/4 Time Signatures.
- 2/4 Time Signature groups the notes into measures of 2 beats. Count: "One, Two" for each measure.
- 3/4 Time Signature groups the notes into measures of 3 beats. Count: "One, Two, Three" for each measure.
- 4/4 Time Signature groups the notes into measures of 4 beats. Count: "One, Two, Three, Four" for each measure.
- Below, are examples of sets of four measures in 2/4, 3/4, and 4/4.
- Count aloud and clap on the first beat for the exercises below.

See Video Lesson 3

Example 1: 2/4 Time Signature
Try Clapping on the X: On the First Beat.

$$\frac{2}{4}$$

1	2	1	2	1	2	1	2
X		X		X		X	

Example 2: 3/4 Time Signature
Try Clapping on the X: On the First Beat.

$$\frac{3}{4}$$

1	2	3	1	2	3	1	2	3	1	2	3
X			X			X			X		

Example 3: 4/4 Time Signature
Try Clapping on the X: On the First Beat.

$$\frac{4}{4}$$

1	2	3	4	1	2	3	4	1	2	3	4	1	2	3	4
X				X				X				X			

Lesson 14: Counting along with 3-Note Songs (LH) in 3/4 Time

- Try counting aloud (123) for each measure, while playing these songs. The songs are all in 3/4 Time Signatures (which can also be called "3/4 Time"). The songs use the notes A, B, and C in the left hand ("LH"): Fingers 3, 2, and 1. *Have fun!*

See Video Lesson 3

For Video Lesson 3, type "Little Piano Book" into Youtube.

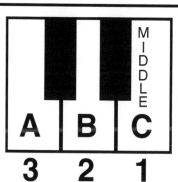

Notes:
Finger Numbers:

A	B	C
3	2	1

*The Numbers in these songs are for the <u>Beats</u>, <u>not</u> the Finger Numbers.

Waltz in A Minor

Beats:

3	1	2	3	1	2	3	1	2	3	1	2	3
4	C	A	A	C	A	A	B	A	A	C	A	A

Falling Leaves

Beats:

3	1	2	3	1	2	3	1	2	3	1	2	3
4	A	B	C	A	B	C	B	A	B	C	B	A

A Memory

Beats:

3	1	2	3	1	2	3	1	2	3	1	2	3
4	C	B	A	C	C	C	B	B	B	C	B	A

Lesson 15: 5-Note Songs for the Left Hand (LH)

- Let's add 2 new notes for the left hand ("LH"): F and G.
- F will be played with the 5th finger (Pinky Finger).
- G will be played with the 4th finger (Ring Finger).

LH

Notes: **F G A B C**

Finger Numbers: **5 4 3 2 1**

New Notes

- These 2 songs are in 3/4 time (or "time signature").
- Remember to count "One, Two, Three" for each measure.
- The numbers here are for the <u>beats</u>, not the fingers.

Sunny Day

Beats:												
3 **1**	**2**	**3**	**1**	**2**	**3**	**1**	**2**	**3**	**1**	**2**	**3**
4 C	A	F	C	A	F	G	G	C	C	A	F

A Memory

Beats:												
3 **1**	**2**	**3**	**1**	**2**	**3**	**1**	**2**	**3**	**1**	**2**	**3**
4 F	G	A	F	A	C	F	G	A	C	A	F

Lesson 16: More 5-Note Songs for the Left Hand (LH)

- Here are a few more songs that use the five fingers of the left hand.
- Remember to find Middle C with the Thumb of your left hand (LH).

LH

Notes: F G A B C (MIDDLE)

Finger Numbers: 5 4 3 2 1

These 2 songs are in 4/4 time. Remember to count four beats for each measure. The numbers here are for <u>beats</u>, not fingers.

Cakes

Beats:

4/4

| 1 2 3 4 | 1 2 3 4 | 1 2 3 4 | 1 2 3 4 |
| F G A G | C C G G | F G A G | C B C C |

Weekend Day Trip

Beats:

4/4

| 1 2 3 4 | 1 2 3 4 | 1 2 3 4 | 1 2 3 4 |
| C G F G | C G F G | A A C C | G G G G |

| 1 2 3 4 | 1 2 3 4 | 1 2 3 4 | 1 2 3 4 |
| C G F G | C G F G | A A C C | G F F F |

Lesson 17: Chapter 2
What We Have Learned

- Left-Hand Notes: F, G, A, B, and C

- An Introduction to Time Signatures

- Counting and Clapping Time Signatures

- Songs in 3/4 Time

- Left-Hand Piano Technique

- Counting the Beats Aloud While Playing Songs

- Saying the Note Names While Playing Songs

Check Out These Artists, Songs, and Pieces

- Mozart: *The Turkish Rondo*

- Beethoven: *The Moonlight Sonata*

- Bill Evans: *Autumn Leaves*

- Scott Joplin: *The Entertainer*

- Elton John: *Bennie and the Jets*

Both Hands

Chapter 3

Lesson 18: Keyboard Notes, Both Hands: A,B,C,D,E

- Now we will be playing songs that involve both the right and left hands.
- Find Middle C with both your Right and Left-Hand Thumbs.
- For the next few pieces, both Thumbs will share Middle C.
- These first songs will involve 3 fingers for each hand.
- Gradually we will add additional fingers.
- The Letters positioned above the beats are for Right Hand (RH).
- The Letters positioned below the beats are for Left Hand (LH).

See Video Lesson 4

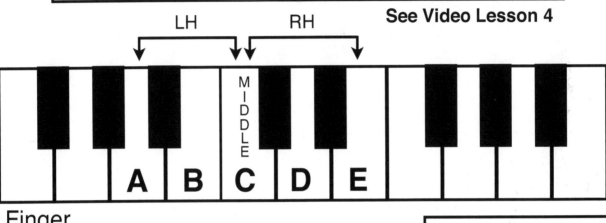

Finger Numbers: **3   2   1   2   3**

Both Thumbs (RH and LH) share Middle C.

*The Numbers in this song are for the <u>Beats</u>, <u>not</u> the Finger Numbers.

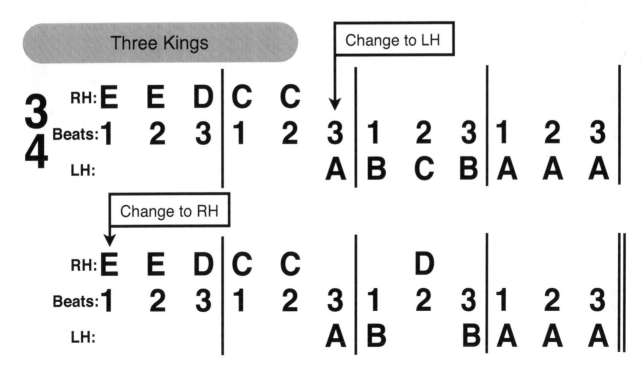

Three Kings

Change to LH

		RH:	E	E	D	C	C							
$\frac{3}{4}$	Beats:	1	2	3	1	2	3	1	2	3	1	2	3
	LH:						A	B	C	B	A	A	A

Change to RH

	RH:	E	E	D	C	C			D				
Beats:	1	2	3	1	2	3	1	2	3	1	2	3
LH:				A	B			B	A	A	A

Lesson 19: Keyboard Notes, Both Hands: A,B,C,D,E

- Here are 2 pieces for both hands. They use the notes A, B, C, D, and E.
- The numbers listed are for the <u>beats</u>, not the finger numbers.
- If there is a blank space, don't play for that beat or beats.
- Both Thumbs will share Middle C.

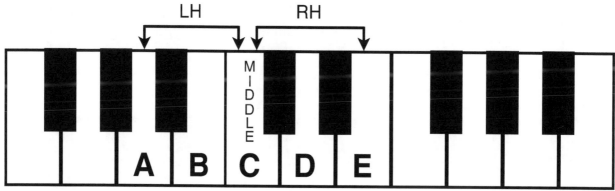

Finger Numbers: **3**   **2**   **1**   **2**   **3**

Both Thumbs (RH and LH) share Middle C.

Beethoven 5th Symphony Theme

	RH:	E	E	E	C		D	D	D			
3/4	Beats:	1	2	3	1	2 3	1	2	3	1	2	3
	LH:									B		

What a View!

	RH:	C	D	E	C			C	D	E	G		C
3/4	Beats:	1	2	3	1	2	3	1	2	3	1	2	3
	LH:					G	G						G

Lesson 20: Keyboard Notes, Both Hands: G,A,B,C,D,E,F

- Let's add 2 notes: G in the Left Hand and F in the Right Hand.
- Both of these new notes will be played with the Ring Fingers.

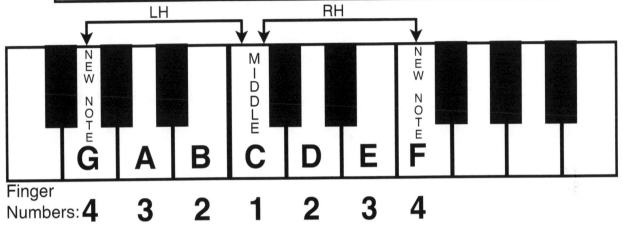

LH   RH

NEW NOTE   MIDDLE   NEW NOTE

G A B C D E F

Finger Numbers: **4 3 2 1 2 3 4**

Both Thumbs (RH and LH) share Middle C.

Yankee Doodle

See Video Lesson 4

$\frac{4}{4}$

RH:	C	C	D	E	C	E	D		C	C	D	E	C			
Beats:	1	2	3	4	1	2	3	4	1	2	3	4	1	2	3	4
LH:																B

RH:	C	C	D	E	F	E	D	C					C		C	
Beats:	1	2	3	4	1	2	3	4	1	2	3	4	1	2	3	4
LH:									B	G	A	B				

March

$\frac{4}{4}$

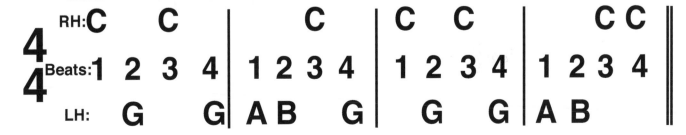

RH:	C		C				C		C		C				C	C
Beats:	1	2	3	4	1	2	3	4	1	2	3	4	1	2	3	4
LH:	G			G	A	B		G		G		G		A	B	

Lesson 21: *Twinkle, Twinkle*
Both Hands: G,A,B,C,D,E,F

- If you see a blank space, don't play for that beat or beats.
- Remember to place both of your thumbs on Middle C.

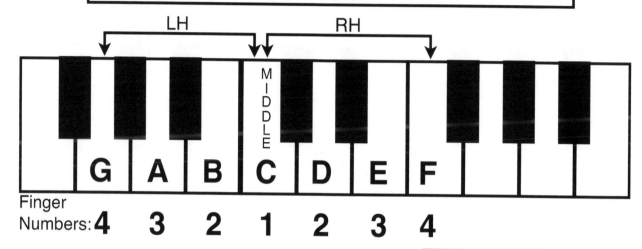

			LH					RH			

Finger Numbers: 4   3   2   1   2   3   4

G   A   B   C   D   E   F

- Try to count the beats aloud, while you play.

Twinkle, Twinkle

RH:		D	D	E	E	D		C	C						
Beats: 1	2	3	4	1	2	3	4	1	2	3	4	1	2	3	4
LH: G	G									B	B	A	A	G	

RH: D	D	C	C					D	D	C	C				
Beats: 1	2	3	4	1	2	3	4	1	2	3	4	1	2	3	4
LH:				B	B	A						B	B	A	

RH:		D	D	E	E	D		C	C						
Beats: 1	2	3	4	1	2	3	4	1	2	3	4	1	2	3	4
LH: G	G									B	B	A	A	G	

Lesson 22: *The Ballgame*
Both Hands: F,G,A,B,C,D,E,F,G

- Let's add 1 more note for each hand: "F" in the Left Hand and "G" in the right hand.
- Both for these notes ("F" in LH and "G" in RH) will be played with the 5th finger (Pinky).
- Remember, the numbers in these songs are for the <u>beats</u>, not for the fingers.

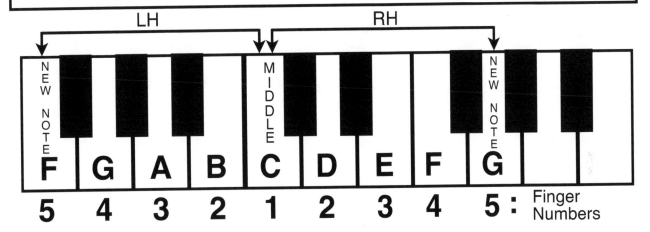

- Both Thumbs (RH and LH) share Middle C for this song.
- If there is a blank space, don't play for that beat or beats. In music, these silent beats are called "Rests. We will learn more about Rests later in this book.
- For "The Ballgame", try to say the note names aloud, as you play the song. This will help you associate the letter names with the keys and will allow to improve faster.

The Ballgame

	RH:			F	D		C		C				
3/4	Beats:	1	2	3	1	2	3	1	2	3	1	2	3
	LH:	F					A				G		

	RH:			F	D		C		C				
	Beats:	1	2	3	1	2	3	1	2	3	1	2	3
	LH:	F					A				C		

Lesson 23: Music Theory: What are Intervals?

- In music, the distance between any 2 notes is called an "Interval".
- Intervals can be played at the same time, for example, if you press down two piano keys or they can be played one after the other, for example, if you play the note "C" and then the note "D".
- On the piano, the easiest way to understand intervals is to look at the keyboard. Play Middle C with your Left-Hand Index Finger, then play D with your Right-Hand Index finger. This interval is called a 2nd.
- Next, play Middle C with your Left-Hand Index Finger, then play E with your Right-Hand Index finger. This interval is called a 3rd.
- Follow these steps in the 2 diagrams below. Use the Left-Hand Index Finger when you see LH and use the Right-Hand Index Finger when you see RH.

See Video Lesson 5

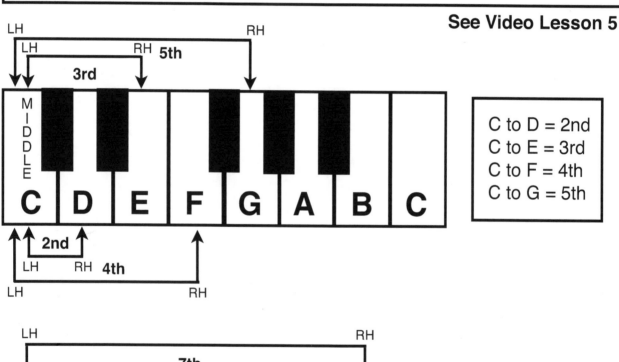

C to D = 2nd
C to E = 3rd
C to F = 4th
C to G = 5th

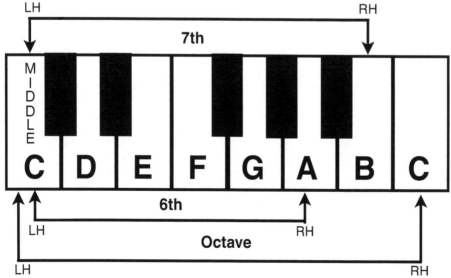

C to A = 6th
C to B = 7th
C to C = Octave

Lesson 24: Both Hands at the Same Time: F,G,A,B,C,D,E,F,G

- In these next songs, we will be playing notes with the Right Hand and Left Hand at the same time.
- When one letter is on top of another letter, play both at the same time. *Have Fun!*

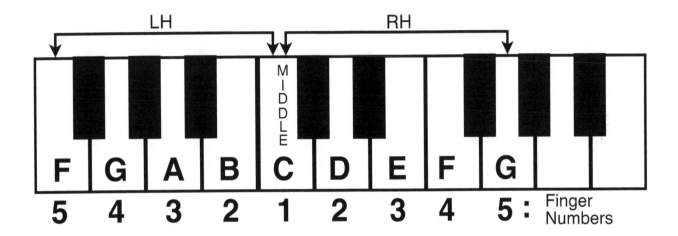

	LH							RH					
F	G	A	B	C (MIDDLE)	D	E	F	G					
5	4	3	2	1	2	3	4	5 :	Finger Numbers				

Fanfare

RH:	G	G	G	G	E	E	E	E	F	F	F	F	E	E	E	E
$\frac{4}{4}$ Beats:	1	2	3	4	1	2	3	4	1	2	3	4	1	2	3	4
LH:	C	C	C	C	C	C	C	C	C	C	C	C	C	C	C	C

RH:	G	G	G	G	E	E	E	E	F	F	F	F	C		
Beats:	1	2	3	4	1	2	3	4	1	2	3	4	1	2	3 4
LH:	C	C	C	C	C	C	C	C	C	C	C	C	G		

Lesson 25: Both Hands at the Same Time: F,G,A,B,C,D,E,F,G

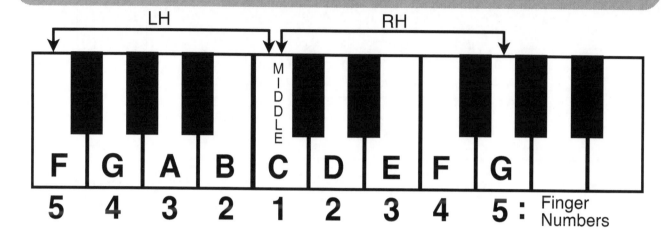

Love Somebody

$\frac{4}{4}$

RH: C E G G | D E F | C E G G | F E D |
Beats: 1 2 3 4 | 1 2 3 4 | 1 2 3 4 | 1 2 3 4 |
LH: G | G | G | A |

RH: C E G G | D E F | E E D D | C C C |
Beats: 1 2 3 4 | 1 2 3 4 | 1 2 3 4 | 1 2 3 4 ||
LH: G | G | G | G |

Snow Flurries

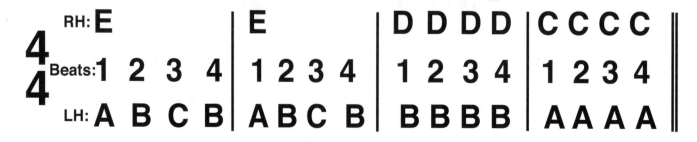

$\frac{4}{4}$

RH: E | E | D D D D | C C C C ||
Beats: 1 2 3 4 | 1 2 3 4 | 1 2 3 4 | 1 2 3 4 ||
LH: A B C B | A B C B | B B B B | A A A A ||

Lesson 26: Both Hands at the Same Time: F,G,A,B,C,D,E,F,G

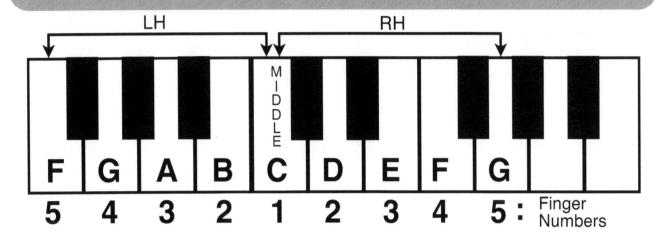

Ode to Joy

Try this more advanced version of Beethoven's *Ode to Joy*.

E	**E**	**F**	**G**	**G**	**F**	**E**	**D**	**C**	**C**	**D**	**E**	**E**	**D**	**D**	
Beats: 1	2	3	4	1	2	3	4	1	2	3	4	1	2	3	4
G				**C**				**A**				**G**			

$\frac{4}{4}$

E	**E**	**F**	**G**	**G**	**F**	**E**	**D**	**C**	**C**	**D**	**E**	**D**	**C**	**C**	
1	2	3	4	1	2	3	4	1	2	3	4	1	2	3	4
G				**C**				**A**				**G**			

Summer Evening

$\frac{4}{4}$

	RH:															
RH:	**G**	**E**			**F**	**D**			**E**	**C**					**C**	**C**
Beats:	1	2	3	4	1	2	3	4	1	2	3	4	1	2	3	4
LH:			**C**	**C**			**B**	**B**			**A**	**A**	**G**	**B**		

Lesson 27: Upbeats & *When the Saints Go Marching In*

- In music, there are many songs and pieces that use Upbeats.
- An Upbeat (or Upbeats) are a note or group of notes that occur before the first full measure of a song or piece of music.
- Upbeats act as very short introductory phrases that emphasize an important note or word at the beginning of a song. For example, in *When the Saints Go Marching In,* the words "Oh when the" are the upbeat. They lead into and accentuate the word "saints".

These Upbeats Start on Beat 2

Do you notice how both of these phases -- "Oh, When the Saints" and "Go Marching In"-- start on the 2nd Beat? These are Upbeat figures.

$\frac{4}{4}$ 1 2 3 4 | 1 2 3 4 | 1 2 3 4 | 1 2 3 4

Oh, When the | Saints | go March-ing | in.

When the Saints Go Marching In

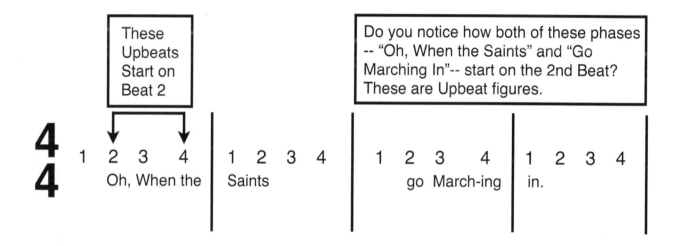

RH:		C	D		C	D
Beats: 1 2 3 4	1 2 3 4		1 2 3 4	1 2 3 4		
	Oh, When the	Saints		go March-ing	in.	
LH: G B				G B		

RH:		C	D			
Beats: 1 2 3 4	1 2 3 4		1 2 3 4	1 2 3 4		
	Oh, When the	Saints go		March -ing	in.	
LH: G B	B		G B	A		

Lesson 28: Chapter 3
What We Have Learned

- Playing with Both Hands

- *Yankee Doodle*

- *When the Saints Go Marching In*

- *Take Me Out to the Ballgame*

- Intervals

- *Ode to Joy*

- Beethoven *5th Symphony Theme*

Check Out These Artists, Songs, and Pieces

- Chopin: *Nocturnes*

- McCoy Tyner: *Giant Steps*

- Lang Lang: *Liszt Concerto #1*

- Lady Gaga: *Speechless*

- Alicia Keys: *Fallin'*

Rhythm & Meter

Chapter 4

Lesson 29: Whole Notes, Half Notes & Quarter Notes

- Let's take a look at some basic rhythms.
- Quarter Notes are notes that get 1 Beat (or Count).
- Half Notes are notes that get 2 Beats (or Counts).
- Whole Notes are notes that get 4 Beats (or Counts).
- In the next 3 examples, try counting on each beat of the 4/4 measures aloud, for example: 1,2,3,4.
- Clap on the quarter, half, and whole notes.

See Video Lesson 6

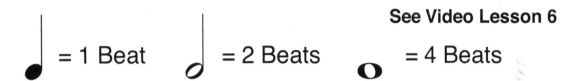

♩ = 1 Beat   ♩ = 2 Beats   𝅝 = 4 Beats

Example 1:
Try Clapping on each "X", while counting the beats.

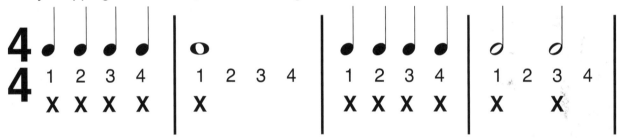

Example 2:
Try Clapping on each "X", while counting the beats.

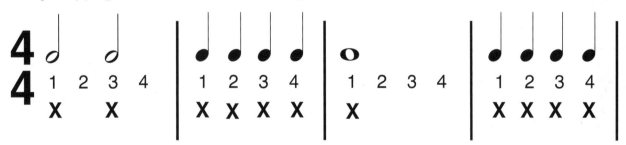

Example 3:
Try Clapping on each "X", while counting the beats.

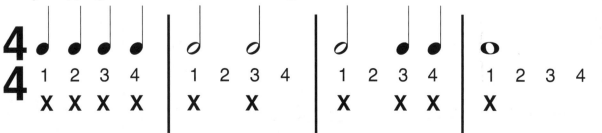

Lesson 30: 5-Note Songs with Half Notes & Quarter Notes

- Try these songs that use Half Notes (2 beats or counts) and quarter notes (1 beat or count).
- All of the songs on this page are for the Right Hand (RH).
- Try to count aloud (1,2,3,4) for each measure.

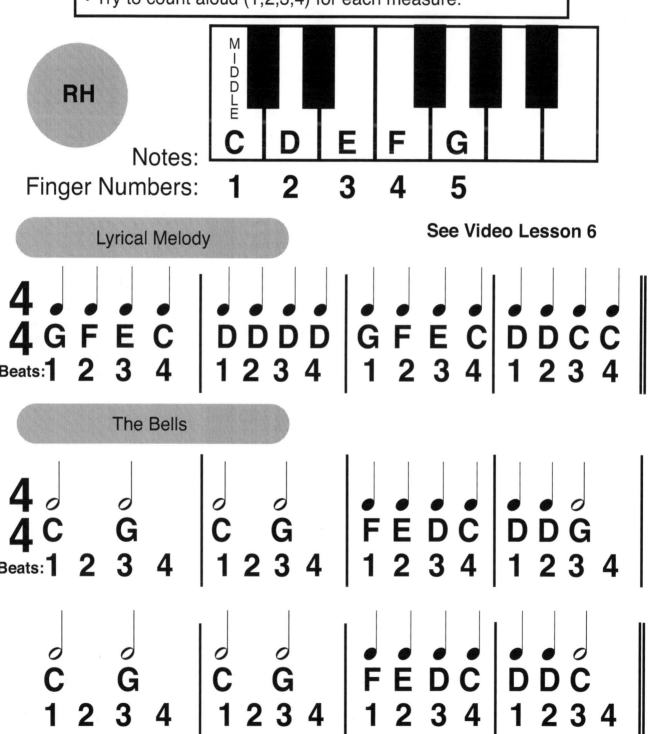

RH

Notes:
C   D   E   F   G

Finger Numbers: 1   2   3   4   5

See Video Lesson 6

Lyrical Melody

4/4
G F E C | D D D D | G F E C | D D C C ||
Beats: 1 2 3 4   1 2 3 4   1 2 3 4   1 2 3 4

The Bells

4/4
C   G | C   G | F E D C | D D G ||
Beats: 1 2 3 4   1 2 3 4   1 2 3 4   1 2 3 4

C   G | C   G | F E D C | D D C ||
1 2 3 4   1 2 3 4   1 2 3 4   1 2 3 4

Lesson 31: 5-Note Songs with Half Notes & Quarter Notes

- Try these songs that use Half Notes (2 beats or counts) and Quarter Notes (1 beat or count).
- All of the songs on this page are for the Right Hand (RH).
- Try to count aloud (1,2,3,4) for each measure.

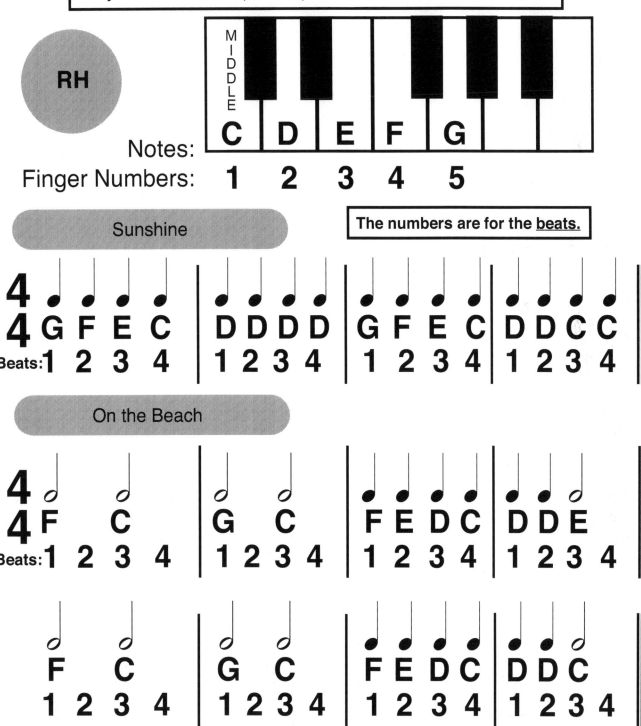

RH

Notes: C D E F G

Finger Numbers: 1 2 3 4 5

Sunshine

The numbers are for the <u>beats.</u>

4/4	G F E C	D D D D	G F E C	D D C C
Beats:	1 2 3 4	1 2 3 4	1 2 3 4	1 2 3 4

On the Beach

4/4	F C	G C	F E D C	D D E
Beats:	1 2 3 4	1 2 3 4	1 2 3 4	1 2 3 4

	F C	G C	F E D C	D D C
	1 2 3 4	1 2 3 4	1 2 3 4	1 2 3 4

Lesson 32: 5-Note Songs with Half, Whole, & Quarter Notes

- Try these songs that use Quarter Notes (1 beat), Half Notes (2 beats) and Whole Notes (4 beats).
- All of the songs on this page are for the Right Hand (RH).
- Try to count aloud (1,2,3,4) for each measure.

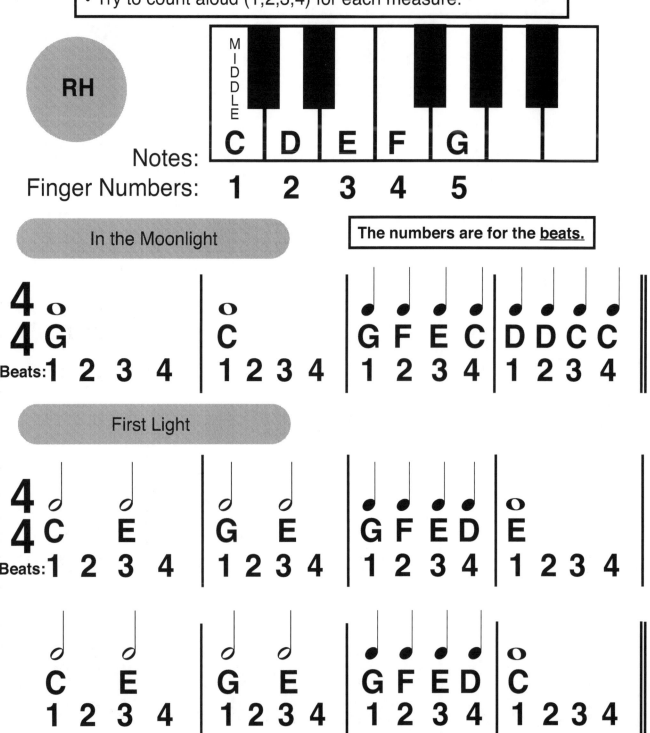

Lesson 33: 5-Note Songs with Half Notes & Quarter Notes

- Try these songs that use Half Notes (2 beats or counts) and quarter notes (1 beat or count).
- All of the songs on this page are for the Left Hand (LH).
- Try to count aloud (1,2,3,4) for each measure.

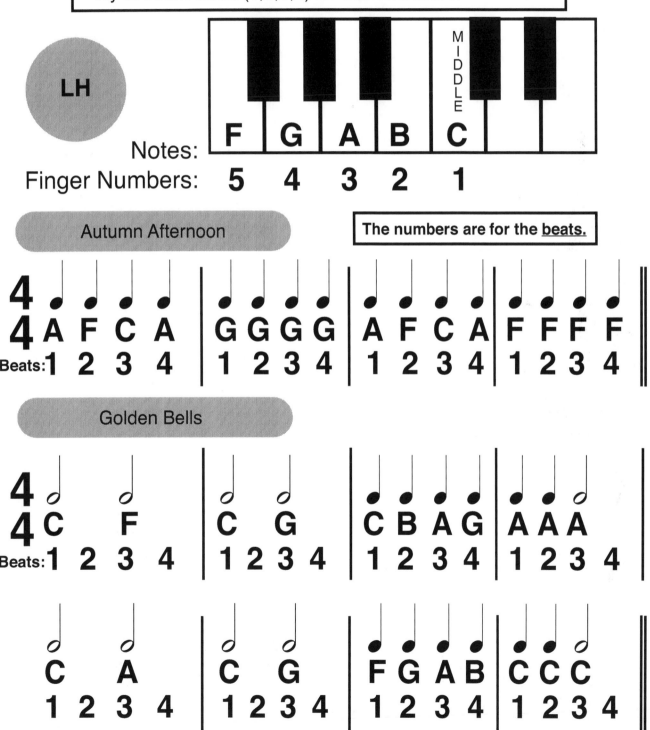

Lesson 34: 5-Note Songs with Half, Whole, & Quarter Notes

- Try these songs that use Quarter Notes (1 beat), Half Notes (2 beats) and Whole Notes (4 beats or counts).
- All of the songs on this page are for the Left Hand (LH).
- Try to count aloud (1,2,3,4) for each measure.

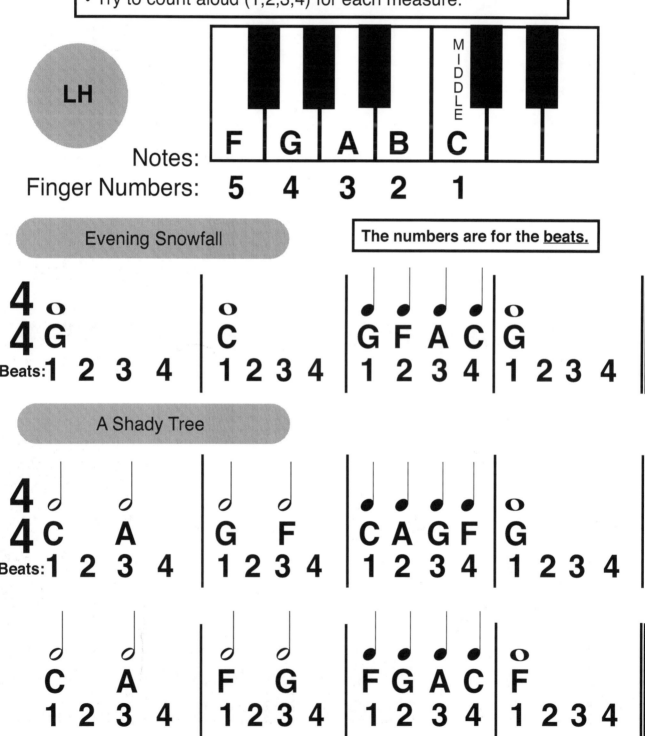

Lesson 35: Chapter 4
What We Have Learned

- Whole Notes = 4 Beats = 𝅝
- Half Notes = 2 Beats = 𝅗𝅥
- Quarter Notes = 1 Beat = ♩
- *The Bells*
- *First Light*
- *Evening Snowfall*
- *A Shady Tree*

Check Out These Artists, Songs, and Pieces

- Cold Play: *Clocks*
- Michael Nyman: *Music from the Piano*
- Billy Joel: *Baby Grand*
- J.S. Bach: *Minuet in G*
- Adele: *Turning Tables*

Great work in completing this book and video course on the basics of piano. You now are developing an understanding of the fundamentals of piano playing: basic piano technique, a repertoire of songs and pieces to perform for family and friends, and some knowledge of music fundamentals--such as time signatures and beats. You are ready to continue forward to Piano Elements, Level 2, where you will learn how to read music, play chords, and add many new songs and pieces to your repertoire.

Keep up the good work and continue to practice and play the piano!

Damon Ferrante

Damon Ferrante is a composer, guitarist, and professor of piano studies. He has taught on the music faculties of Seton Hall University and Montclair State University. For over 20 years, Damon has taught guitar, piano, composition, and music theory. Damon has had performances at Carnegie Hall, Symphony Space, and throughout the US and Europe. His main teachers have been David Rakowski at Columbia University, Stanley Wolfe at Juilliard, and Bruno Amato at the Peabody Conservatory of Johns Hopkins University. Damon has written two operas, a guitar concerto, song cycles, orchestral music, and numerous solo and chamber music works. He has over 30 music books and scores in print. For more information on his books and music, please visit steeplechasearts.com.

Check Out These Books,
Also By Damon Ferrante

Piano Scales Chords Arpeggios Lessons

Book & Videos

Damon Ferrante

Guitar Adventures

A Fun, Informative, and Step–By–Step 60–Lesson Guide

Damon Ferrante

Printed in Great Britain
by Amazon.co.uk, Ltd.,
Marston Gate.